So

Banned

Beat Poems

elliot m rubin

MW01248118

Copyright elliot m rubin, December 12, 2023

Published by Prolific Pulse Press LLC,
Raleigh, North Carolina USA

March 2024

No part of this book may be reproduced in any form whatsoever without the author's prior express written consent.

This book is fiction, and all names, people, places, and happenings are from the author's imagination and are used fictionally.

Any resemblance to living or dead persons and/or businesses, locations, or events is entirely coincidental.

All rights reserved

ISBN 978-1-962374-12-5 Paperback
ISBN 978-1-962374-13-2 EPub

Library of Congress Control Number: 2024901892

Table of Contents

Dedication

To my grandchildren
Shane, Isabelle, Jonathan, Carter,
Alexandra, Melanie, Mollie, and Madison

In memory of my father
Herman S. Rubin
who wrote poetry and prayers all his life

Preface

I believe poetry is to be read and understood by all, and it needs to be written, for the most part, in plain language for everyone's enjoyment.

Too often, poets write in-depth, penetrating poems where you need to be well-read and/or versed in literary minutia to appreciate the poetry. You will not find this in this book or any of my writings. I try to write so everyone can enjoy a few moments of intellectual satisfaction without consulting a dictionary or encyclopedia all the time.

Disclaimer

This book of Banned Beat Poetry is not intended to be read by prudes, political book-banning conservates, and/or sexually inhibited or repressed small-minded adults.

What is Beat Poetry?

Without going into a deep dissertation, it is basically an anti-establishment form of poetry that started in the 1930s and then blossomed from 1950 to 1970ish.

It is meant to **annoy**, be **honest**, and be **gritty**; sometimes in a **hippy, beatnik style, free from sexual mores and manner**, and definitely different than the Roses are Red, Violets are Blue rhyme poems most people are familiar with.

Beat Poetry should **irritate** the **uptight, un-woke, conservative-thinking, smallminded people** in America. One English teacher said to me *if I can't bring it into my eighth-grade class, it qualifies as beat poetry.*

field muse

dusk settles over fields,
tall elms, sturdy oaks,
and round bales of hay
covered for coming frost

                       an owl
sits on the highest branch
its head turns   as it hears
scurrying, rustling below

the muse motions her poet
to sit by her on a blanket
to share intimate inspiration
to be recounted endlessly

with stanzas, sonnets, and metaphors
in page after page of poems
till a bookshelf is filled
with volumes of fond memories

elevator

at the empire state building
i swiped an elevator
didn't know how to run it
properly
up it went
up
up
up
up
up
it stopped on the forty-fourth floor
i wanted to go to the top
guess it ran out of cable
steps are very tiring

closed

the city is dead
skyscrapers reach to the sky
buildings look gray, barren
streets the french forest of argonne
as fog smolders like poison gas
death reeks everywhere
barren storefronts
out-of-business signs
addicts sleep on concrete
homeless sleep-in cardboard boxes
bodies, bodies, everywhere bodies
emaciated bodies
walking dead stare blankly ahead
at nothing
nothing is their future
in the golden city by the bay
opportunities buried in past glories
yellow forward-mail slips are tombstones
taped to front doors
only uber-wealthy live there anymore
in nosebleed apartments   to look down
on working girls who wander black asphalt
in ultra-short skirts and translucent tops while
sirens screech, race, weave in dense traffic
to deal with another tragedy of humanity

highway to hamburger heaven

drive past the yellow m's,
the redheaded, freckled girls,
imperial kings, and the rest of the bunch—
there's only one truly, celestial burger joint

it's down the road   then left by the farm
look for a mesquite wood smoker, smoke'n
on a rural road's sharp curve's carve out
with pebble parking for cars and trucks

you'll smell it from ten miles away, see
an aluminum trailer, a large side cutout, and
old, weathered wood benches scattered about
next to a field filled with bovines and cow pies

lots of down-home folks come from out-of-state
for lunch and dinner   there's always a wait
cheddar, swiss, or even plain old yellow
double sliced, slapped, on fresh butter buns

look for small front lawn signs on the side of roads
from four states away with a meaty, red, double h's
point the way with miles to go, many say you'll
know,
you're on the right highway to hamburger heaven

last dance

late afternoon, shades pulled down, drapes closed
room darkened; at seventy-six
her favorite record plays moon river on the victrola
when she hears a knock on the apartment door
　　hello celia, i'm back to see you
a young, twenty-something-strong soldier
in parade uniform with thick blond hair
appears, takes her in his arms, slowly they
embrace, feet move in unison to the slow
romantic music, as she rests her head
on his muscular shoulder, gingerly kisses his neck
as her long, thinned, white hair flows down his back
　　i missed you so much, peter; it's been years
　　i'm thrilled you came back after the war
　　hold me tight, don't ever leave
the music continues to the next song
she sits in her worn, green velour club chair; it
welcomes a weary body– a throbbing heart, acute
pain, too intense to dance anymore
peter dear, get my nitroglycerin by the kitchen table
peter, where are you, my love
peter, need you.
peter don't see you.
peter
peter

missing

i lost it
    can't find it

if you do
    will you return it

no reward
    do the right thing

why wouldn't you
    i would

if i found it
    but i lost it

not here
  somewhere
    not there
       don't know where
i lost it

tuesday 3:42 am brioche french toast

silence
darkness
the moon hides behind clouds
i live at the edge of suburbia
nobody outside–
an hour away
manhattan bustles and churns
all hours of the day

the six-lane highway ends
two-lane rural roads
run through farmland
cows, crops, and horses
on never-ending fields
edged with an oasis of trees

hungry red foxes
compete with hawks
who circle high above
the brown ground below
both seek field mice
for a fresh meal

while rodents
munch and scamper
on mousy little legs
through strawberry vines
and blueberry bushes

awake
i walk to my kitchen, and
open the fridge
for an early morning snack

pissed off new york

everyone is pissed off
f-bombs fly fast and furious
cars don't stop for pedestrians
pedestrians don't stop for cars
six-lane avenues have people cross
in the middle of the street
like spanish matadors in bull rings
vehicles run past, horns blare,
never stop, miss by a hair's breadth;
easily give the bird, seen in rearview mirrors
while they shout profanities
in hundreds of languages
spoken by the mélange

on the sidewalks, blobs of people
ignore each other, no hellos, or head nods,
they move forward, automatons,
each with earpieces; and in city squares,
soapbox speakers preach personal views,
try to rouse feedback, to engage in argument

at night, in the noisy clubs,
strangers dance with strangers
until liquor brings them closer
and family restrooms start some;
never to meet again, except
through blood tests years later

yet it is a city of love when tragedy hits;
orphaned children, buildings collapse, terrorism,
hearts open wide, usually anonymously;
only in a pissed-off city

holy roller

he doesn't sit through religious services anymore
since he felt it boring, unfulfilling, and
institutionalized prayers do not service the mental
needs of his being—
his soul is his possession, not a deity's, who can or
cannot do anything with it without consent—   he
heard dr. hawking, sitting in the rear of the chapel,
say the universe is chaos, there is no god—   eyes
drift away from the alter to settle on a divorcee in a
form-fitting brown and taupe horizontal striped
dress with long brunette hair cascading down,
draped over ample cleavage, who sits in the next
row over—   wish she sat closer, wish he was
single, for only one moment of desire, maybe two,
but the reality he faces is the restraint of societal
mores—   the basket is passed through the pews,
and wallets release feathers in tens and twenties to
float softly down, with blessings until the collection
collected, and a new cadillac, parked in the rear yard
behind a row of tall shrubs, waits for its driver to
count the take so he can feel the service serviced
his needs

city hall station n.y.c. 1963

steel wheels grind on aged iron rails
as they leave a black, unlit tunnel, and
screeches on the turns as brown rats,
filthy from foam coffee cups, still wet,
scatter under the concrete platform's
overhang as the speeding train
races in the station   while pretty girls
about to go to work, stand back
against gray, formerly white,
unwashed tile walls, feet away
from young men with roaming spider hands
who lean against iron i-beams, to time door
openings and try to get a seat
to keep an eye on incoming passengers
while they ignore the knife in their back pocket,
there for protection—
the conductor opens his cabin door,
then creeps into the over-crowded,
bundled, and jumbled passengers
who, on a good day, is new york city happy
to tilt with every turn, they **jolt**
when the train lurches to a stop
at the end of the platform—
some exit except a raven-haired teen girl
who holds tight to the upright chrome pole, and
the young man opposite her whose hand,
just below hers, touches as their smiles talk
and he misses his stop for work

fertility

titillating test tube sex
is the future of procreation
it'll be how folks get satisfaction

cut and dry, now you can cry
courting is passé, every way
no kisses, dating misses or

marriage, and someday
an appointment at the lab
to make babies will be the way

cheshire love

bangkok barmaids are deep-sea fish for drinking
liquor,
always friendly, never shy, they swim at you to cling
lovingly with cheshire smiles while petite hands rub
a man's back, legs, entice them to spend an hour or
more in their cubicle in the back or up a flight of
dingy, lit, creaky stairs to pay for false love at
agreed amounts while drunk at the bar–   on
eighth avenue, manhattan's corner street girls in
short shorts, and low-cut tops advertise to passing
cars, tourists, businessmen who stay at expensive
hotels for conventions and seek a temporary
winter's warmth with women who make fast bucks
for food, fixes, with tomorrow's short future in sight–
young girls in broad channel, queens, give it away in
shanty town cottages as the saltwater waves batter
the shoreline while parents drive buses, direct
crosstown traffic, or help priests who have shyness
issues with older women in church offices after
morning services–   in iowa, fields of long, tall
corn wait for huge combines to harvest crops, but
police stop everything when a naked, young female
body is found just off the road's edge, in a gully
next to the high stalks, the only clue a matchbox
from a milwaukee gentleman's club which closed
two years before, along with a small gold cross on a
chain which hangs from her garroted neck as the
older county executive in charge ignored the death
of the woman he dated last week

madras, love beads, and lsd 1968

vietnam's hot   uncle sam wants boys
too young to die   no one knows why
old men send them   moms will cry
run babe run   or we're done

babe, we gotta run
no more   nighttime fun
the man put us   in the sun
run babe run   or we're done

ditch the joints   ditch the vial
the man he's nasty   he's very vile
get in the car   we're go'n far
run babe run   or we're done

cross state lines   our only hope
we're too cool   we're too dope
he'll try to catch us   he's no pope
run babe run   or we're done

he wants to change us   run our life
leave us alone   we cause no strife
screw the suits   pressed white shirts
run babe run   or we're done

he's getting closer   i feel his breath
if he catches us   it'll soon be death
leave us alone   we mean no harm
run babe run   or i'm done

rooms

in rooms like these
memory metastasizes
to the roots of childhood
where drunk adults stumble
or fight over nothing at all

in rooms like these
where breakfast's a treat,
lunch, a school handout,
dinner, either soup or
cold leftovers
from the diner
where mom works nights
the day before

in rooms like these
i made love to a neighbor
for the first time,
not the last, and
where my heart broke
too many times in youth

in rooms like these
love was elusive
never exclusive
most of the time effusive
it never lasted
except for my tears
which never end

in rooms like these
i expect to die by myself

a fair contest

beauty contest
held at night
lights off
blackness
no moon light
walk the stage
heels click clack
hear them strut
hard to pick a winner
they all look the same
judges blind

bronx party nyc

cars are double parked in the bronx
invite-only guests enter the building

old red brick apartment houses line both sides
streetlamps flicker with a quick blue tint
then a harsh yellow/white light glare down

vip's now drive up, chauffeurs hop out,
doors open, and taylor, alone, enters; she follows
the wife, who wears black form-fitting spandex
pants
and intends to party hardy while hubby is away,
for twenty to forty, while his supporters send cash
to her

music is live, and bruno sings while the
mayor holds court in a rear room on the sixth floor
as hunter greets everyone at the old elevator's
door,
it's scratched wooden walls after many years
whispers past lover's declarations,
while he offers his dad's best wishes

eric and junior stand outside on the concrete
sidewalk
waiting for mobs to invest a few billion
in their nft collection, or invite them to join
afterward as he flies to paris to meet the premier,
except their sister is on his arm

patient traveler

city buses constantly arrive
never on time
patiently i wait on the curb

i count the line behind
slowly   it grows
the street bustles with traffic
trucks crawl past
followed by conga lines of cars
they slither slowly like sneaky snakes
who weave in and out to go forward

no bus in sight

the line grows longer
my legs tired
coins in hand get heavier
dimes nickels quarters
jumble together
my hand wet with sweat
minutes pass
no bus
no ride
the line grows longer

i hail a cab

big schvitz

nobody likes to sweat
clothes get wet
stick to your body
odors smell rotty—
a friend invites me
to a schvitz in little odessa,
near brighton beach brooklyn
filled with short, bald,
barrel-chested men
with hairy backs
as thick as a bramble bush—
they greet me in russian
i know they spoke to me
they said americanski
when i entered—
i schvitzed that afternoon
more than niagra falls has water
then everyone left and drank vodka
i slept well that night
i hate sweating

scissors

cut ties
    she cut **his** into pieces
    then his shirts, suits, socks
cut ties
    with **his** family
    when her man cheated
cut ties
    with her whore bff girlfriend
    who inserted **him**
    into her life
    in multiple ways
cut ties
    with **him**
    in divorce court
    this was the finale
scissors now dull
    threw them away
    with **his** memories

new york city sidewalks

sidewalks fill with humanity
tourists from everywhere   but here–
shoulder to shoulder
they flow slow, slower, almost stopped
 no one gets ahead–
the crowds are like bananas bunched together
while sewer gas mingles with the unwashed, and
rats scamper about to grab dropped food
on the formerly pristine sidewalks
leaving corner waste baskets
unfilled, similar to the empty pockets
of pimps forced to move
from times square to the dark,
shadowed blocks of eighth and tenth avenues
away from monied tourists of bible-belt naivety
who seek hidden adventure away from home,
with a sinful bite of the big apple

relaxing on the boardwalk, august 2023

seagulls swoop down over
exposed heads
try to steal people's food
as ancient wooden boards creak
under pounding vacationer's feet
who enjoy an early seashore stroll
while an occasional salty sea breeze
lilts gently in from the ocean, and
cools hot, steamy bodies
as the setting summer sun
blazes bright during its death
as it slowly spirals
into the western skyline, and
sweaty, tanned, tattooed mothers,
with pierced noses and bellies,
in skimpy sunsuits,
grasp at toddlers who sprint away, and
feel bubbly confidence
which hopefully will
carry with them into adulthood
as i, a jaded senior citizen,
watch from an old, weathered, worn wooden bench
to observe life as it passes me
while i chill, watch, and enjoy the weather

one night in brooklyn

at seven in the evening two of them walked in—
scarred cheeks, bowler hats, death in their eyes
they entered, confidence oozing from strides
not to be trifled with, picked out a chair to sit,
they bought a dining room, with cash, then took it

big bills in the left pocket, twenties, tens in the right
lucifer's helpers need to eat, their being instills
fright
one tall and lanky, the other short, stout, solid, they
seeped into brooklyn from the underbelly of
society
leaving broken bones, homes, and mayhem in their
wake; faces seared in memory never to be forgotten
not often a person survives fallen angels of
destruction

on sunday family dinner prayers are said around the
table they bought; children laugh, parents honored,
and served first, parish priest invited, business
never mentioned, buried in silent conversation like
the bodies they worked on.

endless legs

he notices
a tall woman
at the other side of the bus stop
next to the token machine;
with pink-painted toenails which
hang slightly over coral cork sandals–
turns him on,
his eyes follow her tan legs up
toned, long, firm stalks;
she wears a short pink pattern
miniskirt,
hides paradise
where legs smoothly end
frustrates him–
only one bottle of amber brew
waits on a table
    in the flea-bag apartment
he rents over the used clothing store
brings relief about midnight
and encourages him
to call pamela, the local bar girl–
she always comes and
leaves her bed when he calls,
love is strange–
she turns on the window air conditioner
by his bed
before they heat up the room
with his trip to heaven,
along her short, stubby, shaved legs,
to tamper his lust–
afterward, he gives her a bus token since
he walked home to dissipate energy

nighttime 3:32 am

deep rem sleep over
decide to write
creativity flows like an open faucet
then i look out my window

the lady across the court
vacuums her floor
naked
she walks back and forth

like the morning dew
when the hot sun rises
my creativity evaporates
i decide to undress

put my pen down
stand by the window
to watch her
when she spots me

she smiles and waves
stops the vacuum,
walks to her window
lowers the shades

on the ceiling of love

here lies love
at the intersection of
temptation and hormones
where morality flounders and
self-control wavers
then flickers
like old, thin, filament lightbulbs
in their last seconds of life

thought you were an LED bulb
never burned out
always ready to turn on
unfortunately
you were gone
when i wanted you

who unscrewed you
took you
from a permanent socket   and
left a huge hole in my ceiling

old men tattoos

viral youth   fearless
never back-off
a challenge or dare
they travel the world
to see it all
barrel-chested and muscled,
chiseled features,
a full head of hair,
wherever they go places,
and the girls loved,
were inked on their bodies
sometimes in full color

nearing eighty
their flexed strength sags
a bald dome exposed to the sky
proud blue eagles once on their chest
now droop down, wrinkled, its energy sapped
emily, annie, terri and christi
memorialized on their arms
are now only memories
of youthful indiscretions
while their wheelchairs brought inside
as the sun sets in the west and
the nurse lowers the shades
for one final time

old ladies on a bus

the casino bus makes its last stop
on the way to atlantic city
seats fill quickly with ten-dollar vouchers
bagged lunches with seniors
on their excursion for the week

curved spines, pressure stockings,
flat heels or cheap sneakers,
some have canes for balance
as they bounce along the parkway   they
head south to tinny bell-ringing casinos
with ocean air filling cigarette-smoked lungs
while they slowly stroll the boardwalk

weary from life
most have hidden stories
but will bury their secrets with them
youthful indiscretions, husbands tossed aside,
some kept, like comfortable shoes
in the back closet
children hidden in sin   never spoken of
until they appear one unknown day in the future
with a dna test in their hands

they don't care where they go
as long as they have their coins
and a bus ride to the jersey shore
these ladies roll along life's journey

gunnison beach 2023

missed it again this year
found out it was yesterday
this was an organized event
i would have tried to attend

ever since a teenager in brooklyn
this is something i really wanted to do
two hundred naked beach bathers bearing all
held up a colorful, bold banner that read

skinny dip day with their nude bodies
blocked out in baby blue ink in pictures
stirred memories
of an unchecked bucket list item

maybe next year
if the waters warm
if the sun is hot, and
if someone reminds me, maybe

free the elves

somewhere
a colony of little people
are held captive by a chubby,
red-suited man and his bubbly,
overweight, cake-baking, white-haired,
swill of a wife who maintains their
strict work schedule, and
enforces sing-alongs while they toil
twenty-four hours a day   with no stops

they're not allowed to leave
on a flying sled
led by an illuminated reindeer nose
like the heavy-set man
while he's dressed in red all day
from head to toe, he ho ho hos
as he sits in a humongous sleigh

then flies around the world
in one night
to give out the handiwork
of his enslaved elves
                for free
while he receives
adoration from children
who don't know the truth
about non-union slave labor
who made their gifts
as they cheerily play
every christmas morning, or
when the mrs fluctuates with a younger elf
in a darkened broom closet after lunch

fish market

senior night at the clubhouse
fills up early with singles
the men have years of experience
fishing, though many
are decades out of practice

the object of the night
is to land a fish to take home
they are all sizes, from petite minnows
to flat flounder and rounded tunas
all squeezed together in a tight school
on the dancehall parquet floor
as they try to lure fishermen
to throw their best lines at them

the fish shimmy around the pond
their tails shake, red lips puckered up,
eager to bite into a lure
as the sportsmen continuously cast
their stale bait into the water

reality is if a catch is made,
and the evening wears on
everyone says goodnight
then goes home alone
to be in bed by eight;
exhausted from tension
due to anticipation

suburban swingers

he's the third car
in a two-car garage
it wasn't meant to be
for anyone else to see
secretive and hidden
their love forbidden
he tried to end and leave
but the others didn't believe
then one day
a fourth car squeezed in
the garage now filled with sin

neighbors complained

two decide to back out
they left without a shout
place seems very empty
they thought they'd call me
i do the math, and
two plus one equals me   as three
but i'm married, and four is not odd

then everyone decides
maybe it's time
we all move to california

wasted life

he doesn't want to be there
the choice faced is five years in jail
or two here at war
not a fair question

if he stays and obeys
his grass seeds may never be sown back home
the stalks will never grow or reproduce
the lineage ends
in the no man's land of wasted lives
eventually, this madness will end

drafted   into battle
bullets   whiz by his ear
branches   snap off
puffs of dirt dust up in the air

he will be a marker on the ground
                  somewhere
where   strangers will look down
                  read his name, and
never know his love and fears

a hill country get-together visit

the party starts in the backyard
past the fire pit and old tobacco shed
where the tree line starts
a swift-flowing creek is behind
the mesquite firewood smoker and
a charcoal heated grill in case
water is needed for an emergency

three beer barrels are tapped
music comes from a portable player
as thunderclaps are heard over
in the next county, lightning flashes
can be seen behind tall pines, when
everyone decides to come inside
except bucktooth clyde, who is cooking

guests free flow into the cabin
coagulate in the far corner
of the living room, except for clara,
bucktooth clyde's wife, who goes upstairs
to look for a towel to dry her husband off
when he'd come in later; her neighbor
billy joe simpson tags along to help

about an hour or so later they're successful
find two towels, then come back down when
the thunderstorm blows away, clyde walks in
with dry-rubbed smoked briskets, prize-winning ribs
smothered in his tasty sauce, mixed meat burgers,
dozens of hotdogs and toasted rolls

dead family

my gay dead cousin is dead
he wasn't always dead
yet he was always gay
plums can become prunes
sweet boys become gay men
sometimes wrinkled, out of shape
with a huge pit inside, which is
hard to take out, impossible
to digest or chew
my gay cousin was a prune
never a juicy plum
easy to taste
he was a prune you had to take
small bites of
but take too much prune, and
eventually, you have the runs
although
they do have a purpose in life, too
as did he

cyclist

my car
stops at the corner
about to turn right
when an old lady on a bicycle
whizzes past me
going the other way

strands of gray and blond hair
flay in the wind
peeks out from under a black helmet
as blue pedal pusher slacks
pounce pedals round
in a *blurred whirlwind of speed*
on an empty rural road

large antique aviator goggles
hide thick round glasses,
as suntanned creviced skin
bloats out like sails on a skiff
against the wind;
the mirage of a cyclist,
like an oasis in the desert
soon disappears
to a place unknown

just desserts

lucifer is busy today cleaning house, he
commands the tortured souls of purgatory
to make space for new arrivals due soon

his handiwork on earth is fulfilling
wars, famine, inhumane suffering
despicable minions listen to his orders

with much glee, the angel of death
descends with gusto to do his job
when he sends the maladjusted to flames

unfortunate innocents rise to heaven
their pain extinguished, forgotten, sutured,
never to return, they luxuriate amongst clouds

poetic passions

women of the night sell passion
poets passionately publish poems
only one passion pounds out money
unfortunately, it's not the poets

luxuriating experience

i'm naked in bloomingdales
in the men's changing room;
a suit hangs on a wall hook
while the door hook
      loops
into a side steel circle
to lock out society on the other side
and salesclerks, too

alone, the mirror, and i
      stare/stare
at each other

intoxicated
with the knowledge
no one knows how i look nude
in midtown manhattan
as tens of thousands parade past
on third avenue
dressed in common cloth
while i hold an expensive designer suit
in my hand
soon to be on my body
when my skin will feel
unworldly supple textures
the wealthy are aqua tinted

after, i rehang it, dress, and leave

alone

night time's hidden love
one's unholy ecstasy
a most joyful sin

delicious temptress

it is a fairytale establishment
hidden on a manhattan side street
amongst homeless and newly elite
chocolate everywhere i look
behind the glass front counter
are donuts, eclairs, cupcakes, and
the queen of indulgence
a cake,
not an ordinary cake
but the richest,
densest,
tastiest,
chocolate cake one can bake

a true blackout cake   with
chocolate cake crumbs crumpled
on the top and sides
my hand reaches deep into my wallet
price is not an issue
boxed
i take it home
with a quart of ice-cold milk

a thick slice of delight
my mouth waters at the taste
nothing goes to waste
i lick the plate clean

truth

poets poem
writers write
painters paint
whores whore
none make money
compulsions not denied
it's a way of life

donuts and o.c.d.

when in a supermarket
i become an unpaid employee
cans, jars, and boxes askew
cause me to line columns up
my mind needs to make'em neat

my wife shops and leaves me
at the assorted, unboxed donut case
where you can't touch unless you buy
i even out the rows, put them in a go-box,
neatly, then place it in my shopping cart

the ones i like
are a little heavier on my tongue
gives me something to chew on
the air-lite ones feel overpriced

vanilla, chocolate, and strawberry,
or really any berry flavor,
even a plain glazed will do
but i have to pay for them quickly and leave
before my wife sees how many i bought,
on occasion, this makes her distraught

especially if she opens the car trunk

waiting

at every baby's birth
the long, cold fingers
of the angel of death
strong as steel forceps
grasps the incoming infant
to assist in welcoming
an eventual soul
into the world
to either prosper or not;
it doesn't matter as
all babies end up dead,
the problem is when—
is it in youth, adulthood, or
as an elderly person   and
what have they done in life—
did they barely survive
or did they achieve,
in truth, does it really matter

tomorrow will always come
yesterday will be gone
today is fleeting
everything is a memory
eventually forgotten

fingered

he was fingered
the bitch's a snitch
too late
to finger her back
that door is no more

my first kiss with lolita

at nineteen
it wasn't her first
she's been around the track
a few times

i could tell

she was the driver
she knew what to do
she is a giver
i, a receiver, at forty
    enjoyed the fruits
    of her sexperience

who willingly kissed me
                    for the first time
to start our affair

drinking companions

after midnight   they left
the dark dangerous dive bar
to check-in
at a rundown downtown hotel

with his miss america
drinking companion
they ignored faded yellow shades,
stained carpet, peeling wallpaper;
they lusted till dawn   exhausted

next morning her perfect skin
rubbed off on the pillow,
spider line eyes flowed
into deep facial canyons;
the bountiful breasts
the night before now
sagged, flattened   a memory
in morning's sober glare

he looks carefully,
his seventy-proof beauty queen
from the evening before
now
a diluted english morning tea
who calls him   daddy

manhattan art class

in front
the art class has a small stage
a black-painted background wall
and a small walnut bentwood chair
to sit on without other props—
easels are set, canvas in place,
students ready to start
a young woman enters

wears a light blue, thick velvet robe
steps on stage, drops it to the floor—
spotlights cast side shadows
on her body as she sits motionless
for forty minutes
a blank stare on her face
as pencils furiously sketch outlines
to be painted later
when colors are mixed

when time is up,
she walks to each student
to inspect
only positive comments,
leaves the room to dress
and meet her lover for lunch

lunch 1962

mother signed me up one summer
at n.y.u. for a weekly speedreading course—
after class, in the west village,
i'd go for lunch at a small, greasy spoon
for a quick burger and fries
when this girl
who spoke with a heavy german accent
asked if she could join me

her dark, wet, shoulder-length hair
offset her beautiful wolf-grey eyes—
she wore a too-tiny tee shirt with no bra,
silver short shorts, and was neither fat nor thin,
with unshaven arms and legs

in brooklyn none of the girls looked like this,
she was cute, and flirty, an older exchange student,
she asked if i would like to hang out after we ate;
i didn't need to speedread where this was going

i took the raw onion off the bun, spread the ketchup
thinly, and asked for tea with lemon after we ate,
i wanted to bite down on citrus after

that summer, i looked forward to speed reading
class
in the city

pizza parlor pangs

near fourteenth avenue and 86th
a side street simmers red at night
a flashing bright neon sign
screams *pizza pizza*
while inside, a dozen small
white tables are jammed together,
as highly teased hair and ostentatious jewelry
sits packed elbow to elbow
inhaling the next table's overdone cologne

at the last table in the place,
way back, a short shapely waitress
who reeked of garlic
spoke to me,
a broad brooklyn banter,
sits me near a rear kitchen door

i can see, a front counter, by the entrance,
a delicious-looking cutie pie,
red tomato cheeks,
bright white moot-za like teeth aligned perfectly,
with a robust yet satisfying
thick overload on top
stomach pangs stir my hunger–
she's a luscious
saucy, spicy meal sitting there
that i too, also desire to eat

published in *Fine Lines Journal* (summer 2023)

a kiss remembered

two close friends went separate ways
after high school graduation
one left for new york to model
fashion was kind to her

she starts to rise in the couture world
unique designs are featured in trade papers
only the best stores carry her clothes;
while alone, her girlfriend enters a convent

taught religion in parochial schools
did volunteer work in the local community
a life of charity and poverty
dressed in basic black, her fashion statement

years later, the fashion icon's mother dies
and she flies back for the funeral and, later,
alone in her childhood home, a nun enters
to pay a condolence visit to an old friend

both of them are now dressed in black
recognition brings a flood of feelings; they
hold hands and gently touch each other's face;
finally, a kiss, lingering, tender, years disappear

lights turn off, shades drawn,
doors locked, old friends, old feelings,
old memories flare up
flames rekindled by undying love

a man of import

money, property, servants
all gone from a recession, now
reduced to a restrained position
subservient to other's wishes—
he saw her look up at him
from her handbag

now, she's a wealthy man's wife
who walks through town, bored,
shops to keep herself occupied-
he is a store clerk in a former
competitor's company
earning just enough
as she enters, sees him, and
rekindles old embers

she remembers years ago
they were others' spouses;
secretly met for mutual benefit
on wednesday afternoons;
when **he**
desired **her**

                        away
                        from prying eyes
she's a woman of import
he's the submissive lover
whose whims and fetishes
whenever **she**
desires **him**

exposed

a young man
went to early mass
went to late mass
read john, luke, matthew, and mark

ignored salinger, hefner and jacqueline susann
studied his bible morn till night
neither drank nor smoked
tried to be a virtuous man

until one day, his eyes met hers—
magdelina his undoing
seduced
    from the priesthood

710 ashbury[1]

the musical dead lived there
strong maryjane
        it's not a mildew smell
with the mildest mind-melt smoke
lsd rainbow-trip laced tours taken,
in and out of reality realms,
concentrated colorful clouds
abound on acid nights—
time did not exist
earthy, imagined sienna snakes
strung on drug-fueled guitar necks
as rock plays on and on forever
beyond sunrise—
wars aren't fought on smack,
they're decided by long night talks by
ginsburg, kerouac, and jerry,
sadly
never discussed with me

---

[1] address where Grateful Dead lived in San Francisco

backwater bayou blues
(inspired by a Creedence Clearwater Revival
documentary)

momma, where are you
i need you;
night is coming for me
daylight fades away—
bank wants the car
mortgage ain't paid
love don't love me no more
it was other girls i cheated with,
or maybe the cow dried up,
who knows—
church turned its back,
said i didn't believe enough
wants more on prayer days

poppa left years ago
never saw him again,
ran off with our money and
that tiny tit town tramp
with five fat fugly kids—
can't remember
what he looks like,
southern comfort erased him;
my pain dulled, almost gone,
i need you
momma   where are you

some call her

a bisexual lipstick lesbian
she flips both ways some days
it depends if she wants to fem up
maybe to attract another woman

the butch girls always go crazy
when she walks into clubs to play
their eagerness feeds her ego
wants them to think she's easy

every night, never alone
always on a pink lady's phone
to someone, she calls too often,
he stays over all night till dawn

some want her to make up her mind
ten years, he enjoys being with her kind
in no rush to change her lifestyle
with patience, he'll love her meanwhile

take a whack

at every baseball game
a batter stands at home
taps cleats clean, waits,
takes a whack

the young, shy boy
goes to the school dance
with friends, sees a girl he likes,
is nervous to ask her to dance,
takes a whack
and asks

a young, tattooed girl
leans against the pennsylvannia hotel
in manhattan;
she wears black spandex pants and
a braless see-through pink top
when a gray haired man passes by,
stops, wants to take a whack
and asks

manhattan windows

like tall cornfields
in iowa
lines straight, row after row
apartment buildings
light up the night
yellow rectangular diamonds
glisten
against the blackness of midnight
while they reach up
to jealous stars

below
unseen sidewalks
fade into a dark abyss
while in residential units
tripoded telescopes
peer across streets
into lit, unshaded windows
become a voyeur's holiday—
where action begins after dusk
as they look into bedrooms of
unsuspecting, uncensored, undressed
occupants

viral shopping

summer of twenty-twenty,
pandemic rampant
people die quickly,
hospitals run out of freezer space
in refrigerated trailers
parked next to buildings,
dead bodies tagged and stacked
funeral homes can't bury fast enough,
but i still need to eat;
at night, after eight, i shop supermarkets
where english is a second language
and spanish laborers, after work,
do their shopping
donde es skippy, is asked of me,
it brings back memories
of a high school class
where i sat next to carlotta rivera
with her tight tops and long black hair,
who would place her hand on my forearm
whenever she had a problem and
didn't know the answer,
but never flirted more than that
so she could continue to maintain
my frustration and anxiety
while she kept my undivided attention—
now, as i walk through
the fruit section of a supermarket
between the apples and berries,
i don't think of a killer virus
but of a seventeen-year-old girl
from sixty years ago
whose smile melted me
into a teenage puddle of muddle

north carolina heartache

i stand on the bridge
overlooking train tracks
in late pre-summer, sweltering june
before the express arrives at noon
to look down at the platform
where i see her stand—
sun is ablaze
sweat drips down my forehead
mixes with tears—
both slowly swiped away
as she looks up at me
then boards
without a wave goodbye—
i offered her
my heart and home;
she tells me
you can't buy love
the ring is on the table—
once the car's door
closes, it drives off—
the locomotive whistle blows twice
its engine roars to life,
steel wheels slowly
grind forward
on rails as hardened
as my love's cold heart

painted faces

times square is full of people
probably too many in a small space
streets are busy and crowded
no rush; you'll never win a sidewalk race

on seventh avenue, pretty girls work
off the curb, always a smile
ready to ask if you want to party with
bright red lips, purple eyeliner

short shorts in freezing weather where
they'll hop in your car and work their trade,
in the din of night, they look pretty good
with painted faces   always a smile

slot machine

it was a little past midnight,
the las vegas casino is busy,
bells go off, free drinks served
seated at a progressive slot
i start to play with four coins
on each pull of the lucky lever
to watch the reels spin 'round
hope for four sevens to finally
stop and run aground—
a full-bodied brunette beauty
sits next to me, never glances over
to see if my machine is hot or cold
until four reels of cherry made me merry—
not the big pot, but ninety thousand
made the place light up; finally, she faces
me, smiles, her too-tight top
barely held her in when she said,
with a smile as she looks at my reels
what a coincidence, my name is cherry, too—
not only did i win a jackpot that night
but the bonus spin too

valentines day 2021

he sits at midnight
in the middle of the bar
to the right of the beer taps—
the vapor of flowing brew
drifts over, inhales,
takes a salty pretzel, dips it
into a mushy, yellowy, cheese bowl

the sound of pool balls clink
in the rear, where a money game
for neighborhood fame and
bragging rights play as a few
women   watch   wait   willing
to love a winner and his cash;
doesn't matter who it is

at the end of the bar, he sees her—
drinks shots, top-shelf stuff,
alone, her beauty freezes men,
no one approaches or even tries;
he sends down a double shot—
maybe he'll get lucky
she's built, long hair, nice clothes,
wonders what she's doing in this dive

before noon the next day, he wakes up
last night's fog still fuzzy
glances at a naked woman in his bed
not the looker he boozed up
but a pool table hanger-on
no memory of how she got there—
because he didn't spend a
holiday of love alone
he smiles

burning man

i remember her—
she wore long, handmade wooden beads
as she ran through the desert campground,
without clothes
offering herself as a trade for drugs
of any kind, preferably strong
hallucinogenic ones— i had nothing to offer her
except for cigarettes and two-buck chuck—
to my great surprise and pleasure, she accepted—
there would be a continuation to this story if we
exchanged information but in the seventies,
we were in our early twenties, and sex,
drugs and rock and roll were all we sought,
no lasting relationship; plus, she had two boyfriends
who traveled there with her—
the week ended with everyone watching the fire—
i saw her again dancing by the flames, again
with only her beads on—
today
in remembrance of a week years ago, i smile

romeo and juliet

the actors speak in olde english
some words are lost in speech
shakespeare
doesn't see my hand in the dark theater
when all eyes
focus
on a brightly lit stage
as my date slouches down

                     in her

                         seat

to watch juliet
give her final soliloquy
with the poison
in her quivering hand
and everything climaxes
at the play's end

queen of los angeles

this is her castle
she is the queen
who rules over a domain
of large cardboard boxes
next to a two-story concrete pillar
under interstate 10 in los angeles—
her protectors spread about,
steel shopping carts form fortifications
to keep out intruders, police, social workers
until the day the city clears out everything

back on the street, she needs to eat
a royal knight, imari,
her protector, sign holder,
begs for cash as cars pass
to throw out coins

he stops anything that might harm her
except when a deadly virus overruns the ramparts
claims her, and the throne's overturned—
the crown's now headless
a royal dynasty set adrift

alone, distraught,
her knight steps off a concrete walk
into the black asphalt moat
when tractor-trailer approaches

the los angeles times buried both,
unnamed, on a rear page

brooklyn beach walk

he walks by the skinny guy
fileted on a beach blanket
and kicks sand on him
watch where you walk, he shouts up
excuse me, are you talking to me
the six-foot-three muscular man replies

in the bible, young david slew goliath
with a puny slingshot and was a hero,
but this is a coney island beach, and
there is no small stone to sling,
only a glock .45 wrapped in a towel
on a corner of the blue blanket

the mouse becomes a tiger that day
and the elephant freezes with fear
the warm waters splash nearby
to silently recede into the ocean's depth
as it washes away remnants of arrogance
until the next day when someone else
repeats the agony of hubris

teenage rendezvous 1963

late afternoon in a summer boathouse
at a rural lake, susan's bare back
is stiff against an unfinished
wooden interior wall as
we feel kisses, desires, and urges
teenagers have when alone and in love
as the water laps against a rustic dock house
while the inboard chris-craft runabout,
inside, undulates in rhythm with our
youthful passion until the boat is hoisted
up on chains, out of the watery slip,
our vertical feet twist in the air
until everything's set, finished,
to be continued at the next sunset
when she visits again
her long hair rests on my chest
to hide our kisses
from the world

drunk'n stunk

what could i say
when asked for help
as i walked through the cruise ship casino
noticed a beautiful brunette woman
in a figure-fitting black gown
slouched back on a burgundy velvet chair
passed out—
her young son stood to the side, watching
as the husband asked me to help lift her—
the clang of coins won from slot machines
made it difficult to hear him,
words were not needed,
i grabbed her under one arm, he
under the other, we stood her up, when
a ships employee took her from me
and they all left the area
to bring her back to her room—
i still can picture the small boy standing there
with a look of bewilderment as his mother is
spreadeagled drunk, a life ahead
to be raised by her

remarriage

music starts,
chapel's rear doors open,
slowly the wedding party
walks down the aisle
as groomsmen and bridesmaids,
hand in hand, approach,
the groom notices his secret
is in the wedding party,
he did not expect to see her,
his secret friends with benefits today—
this is his second marriage, the bride's third
they decide to marry only recently meeting
at a swinger's pizza party—
both want an open marriage
after previous unions ended
because of infidelity
this one will have no secrets or inhibitions,
they thought—
the officiant smiles at the bride
as he starts the service,
only the bride knew
he was one of her two secrets,
and the groom's secret friend
was the other

friday night football

from coast to coast
america's young warriors
gather on a wooden bench
divided by the fifty-yard line

a nation's teenage manhood
prepares to do battle on green grass
as whole towns show up to watch
marching bands march, and
short-skirted cheer-leaders cheer
while hotdogs and popcorn are eaten
until the high school bodies below
dash, clash, and smash into each other

the winner gains yardage,
a brown game ball won,
unpaid prestige rewarded
with replacement knees in old age,
torn ligaments, years of pain,
broken bones and spinal damage

later, at about midnight
a win brings bragging rights
with virginal fair maidens
swooning
to sit in a backseat
with a handsome warrior
to be his trophy

while the losers
ride to the hospital
or go home alone

jagger's lines

facial lines overflow
his lean, thin body dances
the stage isn't big enough
for his moves and talent

at eighty, he struts across it
microphone in hand, to sing with
a throaty, raspy, experienced voice
he never ages   except for his face

rivers of furrows etched on cheeks
eyes still twinkle as a young man's does
his libido written about in rock history books
beautiful women left in his dust

how much is enough many ask
worth millions, near billions
the rolling stones cut a new studio album
they are ready to tour again

memories float

my body floats down
the mighty mississippi of life
it flows past the beached raft
ol' huckleberry used   and
the stories of white picket fences
in st.petersburg, missouri
where my childhood imagination *e x p l o d e d*

i see friends who left early wave to me
on the sloped banks of the high dirt dikes
when further downstream, berms leak and break
allow family memories to flood consciousness
and bring them back to life   in my mind's eye
while not far ahead   i can see new orleans
at the mouth of the mighty river
as it empties into the gulf of mexico
to end my life journey of decades
as i swim one last time

late night

entertainment shows on television,
after late news, bring stars of movies and music
for insomniacs in their homes as they watch myriads
of hosts sit behind a desk to babble about nothing
and ask guests trivial questions

on the nighttime streets of america
questions are asked about which drugs are
available,
or girls in barely covered short skirts,
see-through blouses who look for men
to party with   for a fee

in washington congress wines and dines
with lobbyists' cash in order to influence votes
continue the nation's mass shootings
prevent lower drug prices and health insurance
for the country while they have a level of care
not available to the people who elected them

at one in the morning
crack three eggs, throw in yellow cheese,
eat my omelet in the kitchen   while
the rest of the world descends into chaos

creative engine

traffic flows fast
stoplights slow all to a crawl
creativity's similar
it sputters
doesn't move smoothly
sometimes   completely stops
you can turn the key often
the motor will start
when a spark catches
it doesn't always stop

morning
   afternoon
      night
3 am
as creative gears crank
they turn out stanzas *ad nauseum*
until exhaustion sets in
the engine needs oil
with a good night's sleep

tattooed theater girl

when i left the theater, she was in the lobby
with other girls; as i passed by, her looks flared
like an indoor bonfire to catch my attention

a young chinese girl with flaming red lipstick,
dressed in a white fluffy dress, arms and upper
chest exposed with a low-cut bodice, covered in
bright blue thin lines tattooed on ghostly pale skin,
attractive in a macabre sort of way

out of place in a suburban playhouse
after a saturday matinee of the great gatsby
surrounded by hundreds of seniors in new jersey,
with their walkers, canes, wheelchairs, and health
attendants

her visual eruption drew my eyes
like fireflies on a dark, moonless night,
to wonder who she is: a student, a creative,
unable to comprehend why she's inked up
without a single picture drawn
but lines,
just lines,
twirled lines,
curved lines,
crossed lines
from one arm of her body all the way to the other
arm

mentally, i sought meaning but found none,
ink for ink's sake, and none other
i understand how jackson pollack felt

mountain girl

a barefoot, backwoods mountain girl
walks mud trails to the ol' swim creek
skinny-dips on hot summer days
no tree's too tall to climb to the top

drives fast cars at night with no exhaust
back roads twist, she tears up hills with abandon
speed limits are for city folks; she ignores 'em all
local cops just stay away

met her guy one summer day
had a roll in a red barn's hay
drinks moonshine like a work'n man
hollow legs can store it all

now a senior, grey, and old
porch rocker is her fastest speed
hank williams's her favorite star
plays his songs all night till dawn

progress came and built new homes
fields once plowed now built upon
muddy trails gone now paved over
the creek's polluted, and safety posted

body aches, memory faded, cancer ridden
there's only one place left for her to go,
behind the house is a family plot
saved for her; no rush, she thought, in due time

rage

i yell at the moon
as it brings darkness
while the sun showers the world
with false rays of hope
and fields full of blood,
tired, underpaid laborers
who fled repressive regimes
for sanctuary in an unknown land to toil,
new language and customs stigmatize and
racist, bigoted politicians call them
rapists, drug dealers, and steal their babies
to scatter about like seeds in the wind
with no way to return them to parents—
immensely wealthy pay no taxes while
majority live paycheck to paycheck
bear costs that safeguard our country
while the upper class flies to foreign lands
our military protects with arms and treasure
and our workers' pay for it
with the sweat on their brows,
unrestrained hunger, food pantries beg,
medical needs ignored, women's rights revoked
by the right-wing politicians
until the next election cycle
when they feign empathy
to lie for votes

on being a poet

many use a rhyme-tyme line
to sing a string of words—
i hear you in every verse
oh meter, you're such a curse

my poems are short, succinct,
the stanzas sometimes stink
cause me heartaches, maybe's
when i must cut, delete my babies

did corso or ginsberg bury theirs
with a thesaurus of newborn heirs
those written missed words lost to us
are, but lines and stanzas in a hearse

tiny poem

tiny words
tiny lines
tiny muse
tiny tits
tiny minds–
big assholes
big mouths
big profanities
in a tiny poem
to be censored
by tiny minds

certain voters

the antithesis of free thinkers
    their minds cemented shut
you can't speak to the dead
    nothing can get in
only tiny, chiseled chips drop off
    to fall from their lips
in small, meaningless pieces
    they cannot think anymore
stinted emotions live
    to sprout negatives
although the body thrives
    their lives a dead-end street
mentally stunted, wasted

bus stop

a bus rider asks
who drives anymore

people wait at the curb
the bus passes
doesn't stop

the window clearly shows
people wait
as it speeds past

next bus comes
down the street
a lady steps off the curb

a young man
throws a rotten, bus half-eaten apple
at the front window

splat—
    drips
        down
the bus stops for the lady
she pays the fare

a bus rider asks
who drives anymore
as the doors close

two loves

the singer stands center-stage
in a small, dim-lit basement nightclub
with wall-to-wall
small round tables

wall-to-wall
black and white checkered tablecloths

wall-to-wall
black and white checkered floor tiles

she sings torch songs to her lover
while her husband sits at a front table
listens and smiles

in her heart
she sings for the love
not there
with him, her heart soars higher
than clouds in the sky

volcanos erupt
lava spews
except
he would not commit to her

heart-broken
she sings for her lost love

money

i want as much as possible

too much is not enough

real cash in the bank

not i'll pay you later

or when the check clears

promises don't count

lottery wins might be enough

you can have everything i have

as long as i have you

in my bed

not in the arms of someone else

like you did when we married—

my ship came in yesterday, seems

my lottery numbers won, and you

aren't here to run away with me

like we did years ago to marry

but your sister is

fluidity

he changed outfits twice today already
first, he wore blue jeans with a tee shirt;
then wool slacks and a tweed sports jacket
with tan leather elbows
did he want a third time,
or not, depends, he thought,
on tonight;
his date tendered she was fluid too
maybe a pink dress would be more appropriate,
go as a lipstick lesbian, maybe not,
if she was not butch
he worried about a first impression, and
realized it didn't matter
he had to be the person
he felt he is at the moment—
he/she/they walk into the bedroom closet
one more time
to make a final decision for tonight
there are still six hours to go

in the streets-2023

where are the protestors of the 1960's
when they marched for civil rights and
bellowed anti-war slogans throughout the nation
with the chicago-seven instigating riots,
mayor daley ballistic and red-faced
when his police cars over-turned and burned,
politics were democrats and republicans
who offered different viewpoints
whereas today, nazi slogans once used in germany
are now shouted by a presidential candidate
out to destroy democracy for his ego to survive
and whose only platform is revenge
against those who uphold the law,
and may send him to prison as a traitor,
while he exposes state secrets to foreign agents,
to whomever he wants to impress and
to show how important he still is
after being voted out of office for incompetence
when he downplayed a deadly virus
which killed a million americans;
i ask again, where are the protestors of yesteryear?
arise, **arise, stand again!**
leave your rocking chairs
your country cries out for you

dearest love

my heart cries
when i think of how much you are missed
life isn't the same without you, here, with me,
in the love-nest we bought years ago
in the green rolling mountains of new england
by the gently babbling brook
where we first kissed on our second date
when, you remember,
a young doe walks out from the forest, and
knelt to drink in front of us;
we took it as a sign from above
we would eventually have children together
you were able to pet it
the young deer did not run away—
the fact is you are mine, and
i am lucky you let me love you, my queen,
the focus of my life,
the eternal flame burns in my soul,
my life is an empty container
it waits to be refilled
hurry back from wherever you are
yours forever
                an impatient lover

flower shoppe

the elderly florist
took care of his shoppe
every day
flowers watered, fed nutrients,
pruned to enhance their beauty
with each young flower admired,
looked after and loved,
he knew he could never
bring them home
they belonged in the cold room
for a young beau to give his love
not to be privately admired
by an old man
with poor eyesight, aches, and pains,
who in youth
danced with the pretty blooms
until the sun rose in the east
but now can only admire them
as they go out the door
with someone else

tree huggers

heavy
thick chrome chains
rattle in the truck's rear deck
massive locks rumble around
pickup trucks tumble about
climb mountain paths
with the summit visible
slightly above

when the tree line of old growth starts
their trip ends   slightly before dawn—
when tree-clearing equipment arrives
everyone chains themselves
to thick tree trunks
to prevent cutters to clear cut a colorado forest
for the moment

moments
are short time periods
not meant to last forever
like old growth trees
      except greed
clear cuts through anything
      eventually

dog walkers nyc

dressed for cold weather
susan picks up a dog for its morning walk
in central park at the great meadow
where she partied late last night with her boyfriend
but this morning on her usual route
another female dog walker is there, too—
they smile, nod heads hello, stare for a moment,
realize they dated years before, in the college
dorm room they shared, and lost touch
when california called susan with a recording
contract,
and she moved for money, leaving heartbreak
behind—
the dogs sniff each other
while the two women embrace
as their perfume's middle notes rise
from the neck dabs as they kiss,
holding each other a little longer
only to be pulled apart by the pooches
who need to relieve themselves
by a tree off to the side—
after, a park bench allows conversation,
how the music career never hit big, and she sings
most nights in rundown clubs
in manhattan or the bronx for a few dollars and
free food, while her former lover
became a starving poet, and edits stories
for literary magazines to help make ends meet—
finally, a lunch date is set, and the dating cycle
begins again after many years apart,
this time as a throuple

aging

i didn't grow old
i matured
got seasoned
grew to wait   before a decision
the hustle of youth lost
years ago, not sure exactly where

i'm tired now; naps expected
no need to rush
maybe later
    or tomorrow
    or never
i'll get to it when ready

on life's roller-coaster
people don't upset me anymore
i now realize their faults
without responding, found
it upsets them more than arguing
stupid is stupid, and
you can't unstupid them,
you really can't   because
they're born that way, and
you can't make sense to a closed mind

mick jagger

if i can come back after death
i don't want to be his lips
or sashaying, swivel hips,
nor jumping, stomping legs
if only given one choice
of his throaty singing voice
or a bar smoke-filled lung
i want to be his tongue!
oh, to travel where it has been
a mouthful life of sin
between lips of female faces
plus, other feminine places
i really want to be
old mick jagger's tongue

artic winds

winters chill blows in
tree limbs barren
leaves carpet lawns
in multi-colored hues of death

bird's nests exposed
empty in december
till spring thaw brings back
newly laid eggs and predators

eager to savage them for yokes
while hidden in the undergrowth
bushy tail red foxes burrow down
to prepare for the birth of kits

high above red tail hawks circle
they watch with raptor's eyes
a young teen couple secluded in forest
undress to begin procreation, too

new orleans puritans

a naked body is to be covered
not seen by anyone
polite society doesn't speak of sex

the act itself
relegated to dogs in the street
to be frowned upon, forgotten
as a wayward sinner unredeemed

the currents of lust
float forcefully
down the mississippi of humanity
unstoppable

until it rests in the arms of lovers
exhausted, exhilarated, aware
this moment's not unusual
as one pays the other

for an intimate hour spent together
in private
between two consenting partners
before one returns to his parish

hunting in dear season

run bambi run
it's dear season
the boys are out of school
with summer hunts on their mind
you're not safe from them

run bambi run
they can smell
your essence
want your lips
show you no mercy

run bambi run
instinct drives them
they want one thing
you have what they want
only for a moment's pleasure

run bambi run
let them get you
on your terms, your timeline,
flee until they're exhausted
then you conquer them, totally

why'd you do it abbie hoffman

our country needs you
why did you end it too soon
we had four years of
leaderless leaders
with an undereducated
narcissist
who never read anything

where were the demonstrators
the chicago seven's convention mayhem
with masses protesting
instead, the lambs tisk tisked
said he's incompetent,
yet nothing changed

our country needed you
why'd you do it, abbie hoffman

vestigial

i wake on the sheets she selected
and the bed bought for our union
kitchen tools are foreign to me
never did i ever use them

the watermelon is gone
along with its abundant seeds
i am left with its taste in my soul
and an empty house to roam about

she disappeared with my unborn heir
never to walk the earth with me again
always somewhere, always something
remains to remind me of her being here

mary tyler moore's doppelganger

the high school lunchroom's noisy
hundreds of teens find a table
some with friends, some with strangers
i sit with guys i know from class

across the lunchroom,
i spot her
with her girlfriends, eating, talking,
she is a teenage clone of america's sweetheart
only a few dozen feet from where i am

to me,
the distance between us
is insurmountable,
the pacific ocean is a shorter distance

we never happened,
we never spoke,
she never knew i existed
yet sixty years later,
she still sits there   in my mind
where i can casually write of her today

night

fairies fly in a field of flowers
they sprinkle dust all over childhood
while the sun brightens and enlightens
they hold off dusk as long as they can

in the blackness of evening, they settle in
rest their wings till the morning's dew
the moon welcomes sirens of death
hospitals call, informs of last breath

anticipation, and filled with fright
friends and family dread the plight
everyone waits for morning's light
i am well acquainted with a deadly night

woman with a past

only one person knows
everything that happened
to make her who she is today
and that person is her

the hidden diary of conquests
flames up when read aloud
cause walls to shake, floors rattle,
only safely read in solitude

a woman's experiences are her secrets
building ego and confidence
as she walks into new relationships
with her head up and breasts forward

to brush aside men of lesser stature
seek a hard-to-find man
who can stand on his own
her equal in life and love

boredom - channeling lenore kandel

online in medellin
time of day, immaterial
   they know
   they remember
what internet site
to watch
as naked columbian girls
continuously do it
for twenty-four hours,
year 'round

boredom shows
casually
eats a sandwich,
munches, laughs
as she does her job
        slowly
        then *faster*
two others
roam their hands
        all over
while the world watches

About the Author

elliot m rubin is an exciting american poet who has
been in numerous anthologies and books of poems.
His free verse style of writing is refreshing and
easily understood.

Thank you for reading my poetry

For other books I have written
please visit my personal website:

www.CreativeFiction.net

To follow me on Instagram, go to:

elliot_m_rubin

Printed in the USA
CPSIA information can be obtained
at www.ICGtesting.com
LVHW090056060324
773693LV00002B/222